MW00638145

THOMAS PRADZYNSKI

MODERN REALIST II

THOMAS PRADZYNSKI

BY SAM HUNTER

PALATINO
EDITIONS

MODERN REALIST II

Acknowledgements

We would like to express our gratitude to all the friends and staff members of Caldwell Snyder and Palatino Editions whose continued support and contributions have been invaluable to both the artist's career and evolution of this second volume.

Our sincere appreciation to Debi Green, Director of Palatino Editions, for her singular dedication and enthusiasm in the international promotion of Thomas Pradzynski and his graphic works for the past 9 years.

Our recognition to John Moldafsky, Jeffrey Roberts and staff of Team Art Studio and Wayne and Herta Hedrick and staff of Kolibri Art Studio for their commitment to excellence and artistic integrity in hand-printing Thomas Pradzynski's serigraphs.

Our warmest thanks to Joanna Pradzynski for her unwavering support and encouragement of her husband.

Text	Professor Sam Hunter
Creative Directors	Oliver Caldwell and Susan Snyder
Book Design	Bret Bussey of Bussey Design
Production Coordinator	Stephanie Shedd
Editors	Hazel Boissiere and Stephanie Shedd
Artwork Photography	Almac Photography
Color Separations and Printing	California Lithographers, California, U.S.A.
Front Cover	*Passage du Cherche Midi*, Acrylic,
	51 x 32 inches (129.5 x 81 cm)

COUR DE L'ETOILE D'OR
1997 ACRYLIC
32 X 21 INCHES (81 X 53 CM)

Published in the United States by Palatino Editions

341 Sutter Street, San Francisco, CA 94108 U.S.A.

All rights reserved by the Publisher under International and Pan-American Copyright Conventions.
No part of this book may be reproduced or utilized in any form or by any means, electronic or
mechanical, including photocopying, recording, or by any information storage and retrieval system,
without permission in writing from the publisher. Sale of this book does not transfer by the copyright
holder its exclusive right to prepare derivative works.

The Ninth Circuit Court of Appeals has ruled that removing individual prints or page prints
from compilation books for sale to the public, without consent of copyright holders, comprises
the making of derivative works and infringes the exclusive right of the copyright holders.
Violators may be subject to civil and/or criminal penalties.

FIRST EDITION 1999

Copyright © 1999 Palatino Editions

Printed in the United States through California Lithographers, Concord, CA

Library of Congress Catalog Card Number: 93-072847

ISBN 1-884495-10-9

TABLE OF CONTENTS

LA BOUTIQUE DELLA SPOSA
1999 ACRYLIC & MIXED-MEDIA
39 X 39 INCHES (99 X 99 CM)

INTRODUCTION

t he subtle allure of Pradzynski's works is at once simple and veiled, as secluded and familiar as the gardens of childhood dreams. From his small and modest early works to today's bolder, large-scale canvases, they are urban valentines, in a sense. Yet, given his own history and artistic development, they send their affectionate messages not to a city, and not even to his personal passion for the city that is his ostensible subject. Rather, he reaches out for a universal and powerful desire to find artistic roots at the center of the art world, and he achieves his complex goal.

The hints of past events are everywhere in Thomas Pradzynski's meticulously realistic but atmospheric paintings of Paris, Venice and Naples. The past lingers on into the present, and pervades the most mundane motifs with the elusive fragrance of something or someone not quite visible, but not forgotten. The artist clearly has a special faculty for endowing familiar, everyday urban scenes with a unique poignancy and intensity.

Someone might be waiting just inside the passageway beside "Le Café St. Eugene," or glasses of wine might be set out on a bistro table near the red door of the courtyard off the "Rue des Saints Pères", although the actual human presence is striking by its absence in Pradzynski's work.

DETAIL FROM LE CAFÉ ST. EUGENE

Double doors painted the same fire-engine red capture and hold the attention of viewers probing the mysteries of *La Rue Mazarine*, wondering who could be at home in the pristine garden hidden behind walls on which painted shop signs and weathered posters may yet be seen.

An awning hangs clumsily over the windows of a second-story apartment in *Le Petit Chat*; there is even a certain rakishness and energy in its slightly tipped angle that draws attention to the coquettish lady in the faded *fin de siècle* soap advertisement painted on the stucco wall at the right. The straps of the figure's frothy lingerie have slipped down as she bathes, to emphasize the creamy whiteness of her shoulders and to allude playfully, perhaps, to the partially draped French window. More enticing still is what the work does not reveal, but can be imagined by the viewer: individuals, in modern or century-old costumes, shopping or washing up for a new day with the soap advertised on the wall.

Thomas Pradzynski fell in love with Paris, the City of Light, while still an impressionable youth. However, his passion for Paris, with its historical, artistic treasures and avant-garde energies had to be put aside for many years while he lived in a grim, Soviet-dominated Poland. He returned mercifully to the sights and cultural stimulation that had affected him deeply on his first residence in France, in the early sixties.

For more than a decade, Pradzynski went to school, and as he completed his studies, and painted independently, he was able to visit his beloved Paris only in his imagination. As he longed to return to France, Paris became in his mind a powerful, almost tangible force. Today, more than two decades after he finally was able to make Paris his permanent home, and to capture repeatedly her charming vistas on canvases that grew ever larger as his touch became more assured, something of that youthful yearning pervades and illuminates his work.

LE CAFÉ ST. EUGENE
1997 ACRYLIC
21.5 X 32 INCHES (51 X 81 CM)

RUE VIEILLE DU TEMPLE
1999 ACRYLIC
29 X 39 INCHES (73 X 99 CM)

Even as Pradzynski extended his pictorial reach to encompass in his oeuvre the terrain, streets or canals, and facades of two other great, romantic, cultural centers in Europe, Venice and Naples, he clearly expanded his vision and technical grasp. The restless urge to know the city of Paris that so captivated him during the years of his exile led Pradzynski to embrace it. He explored Paris in every sort of weather, leaving the boulevards behind and wandering into nooks and crannies that seem not to have changed since the visual glories and picturesque architecture of medieval Paris.

Yet there is nothing overtly antique about Pradzynski's Paris as he paints it. His City of Light is a place that appears timeless and ageless, a Paris the world has known for countless generations, from personal pilgrimages as well as from movies, operas and brilliant and touching visual documentaries like those created by the photographers Atget, Brassai and others. The elements of his subjects are well-known: shopfronts in which objects are intriguingly arranged, sometimes with gleaming precision and other times quite casually; upstairs there are lodgings, hidden behind prim curtains or left open to the passerby; gateways to courts that always must remain in shadow, private and haunted with who knows what mysteries, what tragedies or comedies and, always, romance.

In Pradzynski's treatment, however, Paris comes to vivid life, preserving the viewer from the familiar cliches of nostalgia. No one walks streets so carefully rendered that they might be stage sets, anticipating dramatic action, and no one lingers to examine the vases in the red-painted shopfront of *Rue des Saints Pères*, exotically marked with an ornate script that details its contents: "Porcelaines de Chine — Achat." Darkness falls in the passageway beneath a tidy and precise street number, 12, and the placard that reads "J. Martens Photo Studio."

No face appears in open French doors behind the vine-draped window box overhead, or in the windows that flank it. No client saunters into the courtyard on his way to have a photo taken, and J. Martens doesn't show his face. But there are signs that people have passed by, recently and in times so distant that only the peeling plaster and posters on pilasters beside the courtyard's entrance bear witness to their presence.

The signs are everywhere, romantically muted and suggestive. Scraps of paper litter the street in front of the shops, and a breeze gently wafts the flowering vines in the window box, suggesting the fragrance of the blossoms that seem so at odds with the gritty city. Just so do the shadows of invisible trees and the abundant ivy around Martens' red doorway seem reminiscent of other times, and other manners or lifestyles, as the French might phrase it. Quite like the more recent series of Venetian and Neapolitan urban landscapes, the urban imagery of Paris is so picturesque and faithful to locale and visual detail that it could almost be mistaken for an enhanced and enlarged picture postcard.

LES BIÈRES POUSSET
1999 ACRYLIC
32 X 46 INCHES (81 X 116 CM)

LA PORTA AZZURA
1997 ACRYLIC
7 X 13 INCHES (18 X 33 CM)

Yet, while Pradzynski's crisp, strangely intensified and compelling images never shed their representational identity or their nearly supra-photographic clarity and precision, the artist always subsumes his subjects within a carefully organized formal order that remains true to their original inspirations. Their demanding amalgam of painting based in part on photography, and their extremely subtle and nuanced manipulation of pigment, color, surface and physical detail present us, in fact, with a distinctive and poetic contemporary realism.

The approach he refined in his Paris series continued and evolved in his Venetian series. A red boat waits in the shadows of *Via Della Colonna*, the large 1990 acrylic painting that expresses the essence of a seemingly specific corner of the legendary city, its waterways, architecture and artistic icons. And in his most recent series of Naples paintings, while the balconies and shopfronts of *Trattoria Napoletana* are clearly based on contemporary reality, the superimposed central panel and intrusive band of blue suggest that memory and an acute sense of the past are as much competing subjects as is the depiction of an actual place.

More importantly, the tiny squared motifs repeated at each corner of the painting introduce an element of antiquity that enhances its profoundly romantic, even destabilizing overtones. In the cameos at each of the work's four corners, a seated woman assumes a stylized pose, her body draped in robes that evoke the Greco-Roman past, and recall Pompeian frescos. Two other paintings from the recent Naples series, *Caffè A. Lamberti* and *Limonello*, include elements from a less specific past that perhaps resonates with even more complex associations. While the miniatures at the four corners of *Caffè A. Lamberti* and the classical columns inserted so provocatively at the base of *Limonello* recall antiquity, the row of yellow fruits that appear about to tumble down from a dark, cavernous shelf can be referenced both to contemporary life and more current art history.

With their sharp definition, strong sense of order and austere simplicity, the lemons translate not only into acceptable and convincing modern objects but also suggest earlier art expressions — perhaps even a connection to the Spanish Baroque still life paintings of Juan Sánchez Cotán, which they so resemble. Whatever their evocative associations, the lemons confer haunting overtones on Pradzynski's seemingly sunny, open work. At the same time, they keep his paintings vital as paintings long after the specifics of their subject matter have mellowed into a clear, identifiable nostalgia.

The psychological paradoxes that shadow Pradzynski's apparently straightforward but quite complex realism are reflected in the constraints of his personal history. Born in 1951 in Lodz, Poland, he experienced at first-hand the deprivations of life under the Soviet occupation in his youth, when revolution swept through his beleaguered land. Nothing specifically implicating those days of terror, at least in terms of an explicit narrative, can be seen in the paintings and prints he produced so steadily and serenely over the past 22 years, ever since Pradzynski and his wife Joanna emigrated to Paris. Yet there seems to be something amiss in the shadows and flickering light of the shops that are invariably represented as dark and shuttered rather than open and inviting. Furthermore, one finds an equivocal atmosphere in dozens of his urban studies, especially those utilizing overlays of photo transfer. And finally, and most notably, the conspicuous absence of humankind in his works affords reason to deduce that something of a personal past, partly repressed, partly transformed, lingers on in his work.

Juan Sánchez Cotán, 1560-1627,
Quince, Cabbage, Melon and Cucumber, c. 1602,
San Diego Museum of Art, CA (Gift of Anne R. and Amy Putnam)

CITÉ BERGÈRE
1998 ACRYLIC
24 X 15 INCHES (61 X 38 CM)

MODERN REALIST

At Thomas Pradzynski's birth on November 29, 1951, Poland was ruled by the pro-Communist government that had been installed in 1947. By the time he was a year old his nation had adopted a Soviet-style constitution and formally became part of the USSR. His earliest surroundings were grim, in a country still recovering from the Second World War; nonetheless, despite the repressive atmosphere, as a child he exhibited significant artistic talent that could not be stifled. His interest in making art was nurtured by his aunt, Jolanta, and her husband, both artists who lived in Krakow. Between the wars these older artists had experimented with a variety of styles from Expressionism and Surrealism to abstraction, and they were able to expose the gifted child to a variety of formal alternatives while tutoring him in technique and giving him a general appreciation of art history.

Pradzynski's artistic path was further determined in 1960, when his father, a representative of the Polish farm industry, was stationed in Paris for four years. The charms of Paris made a profound impression on the boy, and drew him back permanently to the city some twenty years later. It is almost impossible to imagine the impact the move to France and the four-year residence in Paris had upon the precocious young artist. The family moved into Montmartre, a quarter steeped in bohemian anecdote and myth surrounding the great artistic personalities who shaped modern art. Pradzynski never forgot the experience when he returned home four years later, and he has remained closely connected to Paris throughout his life. Just nine years old when he arrived, he suddenly found himself at a world center, and at the traditional heart of the art world. All around a child already deeply immersed in art were its icons: the beautifully preserved old neighborhoods, the monuments, the great museums, even the proliferation of street artists and the streets themselves, the wandering pathways and vernacular architecture of antique Paris, contrasting vividly with the magnificent boulevards that were shaped less than a century earlier by the Baron Haussman.

COUR DES TROIS FRÈRES I
1998 ACRYLIC
32 X 24 INCHES (81 X 60 CM)

The change was dramatic, and deeply affecting: Lodz, gray, grim and industrial, was relatively small and firmly working class; Paris, simply enormous and worldly, and imbued with millennia of culture, was truly his City of Light. Pradzynski recalls vividly how taken he was with Paris, the city where youthful art dreams came true as he experienced his adolescence, and grew into young manhood. He was captivated by the spirit of Paris, by its tempo, culture and *joie de vivre*; for the young Thomas, it became the center of the only universe he would later care to inhabit.

The Paris Pradzynski encountered was from an earlier time, a city preoccupied just then, in all its heady, anarchic innocence, with a classic moment of late modernist expression, in New Wave films by Francois Truffaut and Jean-Luc Goddard. Paradoxically, he also subsequently learned to appreciate more remote traditions. He was soon absorbed in the historical Paris of Louis XIV, Watteau, Marie Antoinette, and later the Barbizon School, Zola, Courbet, Impressionism and Toulouse-Lautrec. In due course, he assimilated the Cubists, Dadaists and Surrealists, Lumière and Jean Renoir, a full range of cultural history which in maturity he transposed in his imagination into his own observant and romantic vein of expression. The streets, shopfronts and signs of old Paris were to become his first obsessive subject matter, and always remained irresistibly, permanently seductive. From this early encounter, the subject matter of the externals and facades of old Paris was transformed into a distinctive kind of poetic realism that sprang from his mind and memory, as Paris street scenes became his first enduring subject.

LA FERME STE. SUZANNE I
1997 ACRYLIC
29 X 46 INCHES (73 X 116 CM)

PARAPLUIES REVEL
1996 ACRYLIC
24 X 18 INCHES (61 X 46 CM)

But in 1965 the young man was compelled to return to Poland with his family, and there he went on to complete his studies at the Lycée Français in Warsaw in 1968, a year of impassioned, violent uprisings on student campuses throughout the West. This potent wave of youthful discontent actually began in France and prominently included Paris. Pradzynski went on to study art privately at Warsaw's Academia Szutk Pieknych, mastering the drawing skills that today remain so much in evidence in his richly detailed, expressive works. At that point, rather than continuing with his art studies in a repressive society that had no real use or appreciation for them, Pradzynski entered a program of Social and Economic Sciences Studies at SGPIS in Warsaw, and graduated in 1976 with his master's degrees in both sociology and economics.

He had not spent all his time since 1965, when he left Paris and returned to Poland, on practical or academic matters, of course. While Warsaw hardly qualified as a great or enlightened world center, in the late 1960s it was nonetheless home to a multitude of young people who had established contact with their impassioned, restless counterparts in Paris and elsewhere in the West. There was a revolution underway, a universal rebellion against repression and, specifically, against the outmoded establishment mores that continued to grip America, and expanded France's misguided efforts to thwart Communism in Vietnam. The price for black market goods was high, but Polish teenagers managed to express solidarity with the fermenting attitudes of their peers outside the Soviet bloc. They too wore Levi's, raged to Bob Dylan's protests, rocked to Eric Clapton's blues and believed fervently in a better way of life, a more perfect, utopian future that would shape new art forms as well.

This pivotal moment in history had an impact on his life, Pradzynski recalled. "I was a hippie. I lived with my girlfriend, we had long hair, music, marijuana, the same as in the States, but it was different. We wanted to be independent, to be on our own, but there was no place for teenagers to live, no apartments. That was part of the system," he has said. "In a country like Poland, you don't make any plans. It's one of the characteristics of communistic life that it curbs individuality and dreams and projects." [1]

His father had died in 1968, a loss that led Pradzynski to turn away from art long enough to earn his advanced degrees in professional areas, but he did not abandon his desire and drive to work as an artist. While he continued his practical studies, he gradually turned from sociology and economics to art and architectural classes at the Ecole Politecnique in Warsaw, satisfying a long-held interest in the structures and textures of buildings. The purely technical side of his new focus couldn't hold his interest, however, and Pradzynski soon shifted his energies exclusively to painting and to the studio art classes he was already taking at the school. He had begun to sell the paintings which he made by copying icons and adapting them to original compositions. As he would do in his Paris series, and in the studies of Venice and Naples that followed, he began to look around him searching for subjects, an intriguing building, a memorable street scene, and he captured them on canvas. Along the way, he found himself actively seeking the concentrated approach that would lead him to a professional success.

COIFFEUR POUR DAMES
1998 ACRYLIC
26 X 51.5 INCHES (65 X 130 CM)

COUR DES TROIS FRÈRES II
1999 ACRYLIC
24 X 18 INCHES (61 X 46 CM)

At the age of 26, with considerable stature in academic areas that failed, however, to satisfy his deepest urges, Pradzynski focused his energies on a career in art. He and Joanna married that year, in 1976, and they settled in Lodz, as he continued to push his career as an artist. He reveled in his early commercial success almost naively, as much for the encouragement it provided as for the economic necessity, and in 1977 he was able to propose taking his bride to the city that had so deeply engaged him. The couple set off for Paris, planning only a visit, and the door Pradzynski had closed in 1965 reopened for him, in all its richness and vast potential for self-realization. He shared his Parisian days with Joanna, taking her to his boyhood haunts and falling in love again with the French capital, and all it promised.

Time passed, and they extended their stay. Finally, perhaps carelessly and more likely because of their subliminal attraction to Paris, they let their visas expire and faced the reality of their decision: if they returned to Poland with expired visas, they would not be issued other visas to visit the city they loved. They remained in Paris, cut off abruptly from their families as long as the Iron Curtain was in place but surrounded by Thomas's essential wellspring, the city itself.

Pradzynski didn't waste any time coming to grips with his inspiration. He immediately took up his search for the approach and motifs that would best express his formal concerns, making extensive studies of light and texture, exploring compositional variations and refining his inner vision. He painted what would now appear to be naive street scenes, pinpointing the spirit of Paris as he experienced it then, and, more subtly, as he had experienced it as an impressionable boy from Lodz years earlier, in a sort of overlay that revealed itself in the palimpsests that finally began to emerge on his canvases. And gradually his venerated subjects, the aged facades, crumbling walls, peeling shop signs, and rain-slicked streets took on a life of their own, becoming his very personal, unique statement.

His observations and reactions to the Parisian environment, and his chosen subject matter, were acute, penetrating and constant. He wandered the streets as a lover might, seeking solace and reading romantic meanings into every aspect of what he saw and felt: a half-opened shutter; a passageway between shops, perhaps suggesting some imaginable events or an enticing cluster of objects. Increasingly, as his own approach came into focus, and a recognizable style of meticulous realism developed, he became enamored of a subject matter in the context of a particular moment in time. Paris obviously became a very special place for Pradzynski, the beating heart of the eternal Western art world, that opened his eyes to art's expressive possibilities, and helped him define his own place in art history. It was here that he developed an almost uncanny ability to depict the textures and minute details of objects, imitative skills combined with an imaginative vision that soon allowed him to build a professional career and devote himself entirely to painting.

Fabrique de Carrelages en Provence
1996 Acrylic
46 x 35 inches (116 x 89 cm)

Impasse Amelot
1996 Acrylic
16 x 11 inches (41 x 27 cm)

Not surprisingly, Paris itself became his ostensible subject. He studied it not so much as a native, despite his seminal years there, but as a passionate student and observer returning to rediscover the city's antique beauty and current relevance to his art. Even as Paris became his home, it became his mistress, the *raison d'être* for his creations. Convinced that he was seeing an interior, ancient Paris, and concerned that the old Paris was vanishing as progress erased its quiet courtyards and ageless *patisseries* and *boulangeries*, he set out to preserve it all on canvas, much as Atget had documented Paris in the first quarter of the century with his camera. Atget gave his subjects, which were primarily humble working folk rather than their environs, a sense of immutable presence which Pradzynski reserved exclusively for their background of the streets and shops of Paris, with the local population excluded. His early works were

small gems that distilled the emotions and energies of specific, identifiable places. And, like the larger paintings that soon followed, and the manifold serigraph prints that succeeded them as Pradzynski found international success, they focused on locale, on building facades, signs crystallized at first in diminutive form by accenting almost microscopic detail with sparkling highlights. The people who built, used or inhabited these edifices were strictly excluded from his renderings of reality, however.

In the beginning he composed works of over-powering detail, until they literally became still lifes of city streets and meandering side roads; devoid of action, the human presence or narrative content, they nonetheless seemed more real than reality. Although based on photographic models, his subjects were sufficiently assimilated and transformed in the painting process to render them as a consistent, believable whole within the total construct of his painting. As in paintings by Flemish and other masters of the Northern Renaissance, Pradzynski observed nature in almost excruciating detail, and this program of intense concentration on visual fact actually seemed to enhance and empower his imagery, charging even the most commonplace or innocuous subject matter with importance. His desire was, literally, to "romanticize the empty streets and the traces of the past, and to preserve places that are slowly disappearing," [2] he has said.

The mission had acquired a sense of urgency, for the past was eroding as quickly as the old buildings, in their visible disrepair and decay. Pradzynski was eager to advance along the path on which he had now set himself. "When describing my art it is important to stress that I do not try to either imitate hyper-realism or *trompe l'oeil*," he said. "I am interested in detail and try to create an anecdote. I use light by manipulating reflections that come and go, animating the beauty of a deserted street. I am fascinated with big cities like Paris and New York, and from their streets I try to find new visual realities for others to enjoy and discover. I love the past and present in everyday life and I hope to create that feeling in my art. At times I create a painting from a composition of several elements existing in different places, thus creating an image ideal to me. A lot of people see nostalgia in my paintings. It is a feeling I look for in places where life has stopped or is changing." [3]

ARGUENCE LUTHIER
1997 ACRYLIC
25.5 X 39 INCHES (64 X 99 CM)

ARTISAN CHAPELLIER
1996 ACRYLIC
18 X 24 INCHES (46 X 61 CM)

Pradzynski searches for specific sites, and uses conjunctions of different imagery drawn from a variety of places, not just in the streets, but in vintage photographs that set off the mood that liberates his work. His first and primary inspiration, certainly, comes from his ramblings in the quaint streets of Paris, and then, in later works, as his scope and range of experience expanded, he progressed to Venice and Naples. As he developed and enlarged his painterly style, he experimented with mixed compositional devices, including photomontage, an approach involving greater risks pictorially. He used photographic overlays in silkscreen, obscuring another urban image beneath that was allowed to bleed through, ingeniously creating mysterious *pentimenti*. These *pentimenti* subliminally evoke quite unrelated historical periods, drawn from a more distant past.

Perhaps unintentionally, Pradzynski often demonstrates an almost Proustian affinity for visual detail marking the passage of time, and recalling with precision the elusive past. While bicycle racks stand empty in *La Rue Mazarine*, and posters still appear to carry the imprint of a departed hand, they also seem closely linked to archival photographs of turn-of-the-century Paris. The artist collects vintage photographs of this kind, and rather reveres them. Although he never incorporates them directly in his work, he often unconsciously absorbs their settings and appurtenances into his mixed time-frame. Pradzynski does not choose to borrow images from the past directly, since his goal is more subtle, and in a sense more classical. While he is aware of such photographs, his concern is with their manipulation. He does not literally reinstate them in his art. What he incorporates in his work, beginning with his Venetian paintings, are historical markers that permit association with another time.

Furthermore, his depicted contemporary world is not literal, despite its overwhelming sense of veracity. In the 22 years since he made Paris his home and began to explore not just her every nook and cranny but her very soul, he has found his path into a personal, poetic genre of urban painting than can best be categorized as landscape in transition to still life. His paintings are also not direct representations of a particular site, but a synthesis of different sites, facades, signs and related subject matter. In his recent Venetian paintings, images of historical monuments are superimposed on contemporary subject matter, and Venetian facades and shopfronts. By invoking the past, they incorporate time as another dimension accessible to art. Working in a spirit actually similar to Cubism, he reaches out beyond the naturalism created by his skillful suggestion of three dimensions on a flat surface to encompass time itself. But instead of depicting the illusion of time and space literally on his canvas, Pradzynski refers to his subject matter, and its more complex ramifications, elliptically, leaving out such topical elements as people and clothes that would define their era, and other telltale accoutrements.

TRATTORIA GIOVANNI
1997 ACRYLIC
11 X 16 INCHES (27 X 41 CM)

Au Pont Louis Philippe
1997 Acrylic
21 x 32 inches (53 x 81 cm)

And so, as he has moved confidently from his initially diminutive studies and a rather "hard" descriptive style, defined by meticulous detail and academic brushwork, into larger paintings, he has evolved a freer, more sensual style, marked by luminous colors and a more ingratiating surface invention. With these changes in vision and technique he has made remarkable advances in his art. Today the paintings are more technically diverse, and focus on three great European cities, Paris, Venice and Naples. He has created an astonishing series of dramatic stages, complete with convincing illusionistic backdrops, and pathways that lure the eye into mysterious depths across the surfaces of frayed and eroded textures that all bespeak the passage of time. Romantic in their shabbiness, their worn corners and elusive enclaves, these serial but never identical or tedious facades and courtyards express far more than any photograph, or any single viewpoint could engender. They offer multiple perspectives, but not exclusively in spatial terms, as do the images of Cubism. Pradzynski's vistas are more complex in psychological terms. Their echoing overtones, especially in his current

work inspired by Naples and Venice, may successively obscure his preliminary image, shredding its representational identity. Yet in the process of transformation, his images take on additional formal and psychological significance, much like the mysterious overlaid imagery of a Rauschenberg screen painting. They are also contained and held in taut equilibrium by Pradzynski's primary concern for a formal order. The combination of an astute formalism with the command of pictorial detail and the creation of an arresting vision of his preferred motifs define Pradzynski's unique expression.

Robert Rauschenberg, Kite, 1963, 84 x 60 inches
Oil and Silkscreen on canvas, 1963
©Robert Rauschenberg/Licensed by VAGA, New York, NY

le Petit Chat

Savon de Toilette
MARSEILLE

3615 à LOUER
1,2,3,4 PIECES
LOISELET et DAIGREMONT
44 30 45 40

PARFUMERIE

86

clac

BIJOUX FANTAISIE MAROQUINERIE

JOALLIER BIJOUTIER
J. M. De Cassay

PARIS

radzynski mastered his unique approach to painting in Paris, in the series that

began with small, intense studies and expanded to works of larger scale. The

works continued to evolve as he developed his unique vision. In *La Rue Mazarine*,

the 1996 acrylic painting that captures the stark contrast between an eroding, poster-

encrusted wall and the fresh, tree-lined garden it encloses, visible through an open gate, the

emphasis is on rich textures and the play of a soft, seductive light which the artist masterfully

recreates. He even seems to revel in the messy graffiti, poster tatters, and splotches of grayed,

aging paint that cover the old masonry wall. This scene of rather squalid neglect might give a

less resolute artist some pause. But Pradzynski succeeds in turning this partially unattractive

site into a game of painterly puns, a dialogue between past and present, decay and an image

of renewal in the brief, vivid glimpse of the interior courtyard garden. Noticeably, and

perhaps even romantically, the absence of any human beings becomes a nagging factor

in the visual and mental experience of the work. This ultimately casts Pradzynski in

the role of a detached observer, an impartial eye. He seems at first glance to have

withheld judgment or emotional involvement with his vividly depicted subject matter.

LE PETIT CHAT
1998 ACRYLIC
32 X 39.5 INCHES (81 X 99.5 CM)

The impassive fortress-like exterior of the building, its eroded walls, defaced signs and the pervasive gray-brown tonalities create a rather dour reality. Yet one has to admire the simple clarity of Pradzynski's vision, and the fact that he is willing to pursue with such avidity the most unromantic exterior imaginable. He does provide some relief, a moment of grace in this rather lugubrious environment, with the narrow courtyard vista and vivid blue overhead shutters. But the real release, emotionally and visually, comes with the opening in the wall, revealing a space that appears as a magical garden in comparison with the street. There is a certain stubborn honesty in the choice of such a banal motif, despite its dramatic resolution, and the very effort of so diligently articulating its esthetic possibilities can only inspire admiration.

LA RUE MAZARINE
1996 ACRYLIC
32 X 46 INCHES (81 X 116 CM)

RUE DES SAINTS PÈRES
1997 ACRYLIC
46 X 35 INCHES (116 X 89 CM)

In another of Pradzynski's Parisian paintings, *Rue des Saints Pères*, executed in 1997, the focus is tighter, more compressed and sharper, and the formal balances are more precise. The rectilinear openings in the buildings flanking a dark, narrow passageway into the photography studio of J. Martens, as the observer learns from an overhead sign, are very different from one another, enhancing visual interest. On the right, washed with warm light and implied motion, is the awning-hooded display whose wares are a vivid blur; to the left, in a smaller vertical vitrine, are the fragile vessels imported from the orient, "Porcelaines de Chine — Achat," as the painted text on the polished window notes.

The absolute exquisiteness of the porcelain display, however, isn't the whole story; Pradzynski interweaves his imagery more interestingly, and with more complexity, by placing an old tattered poster on the jamb between the gateway and oriental display in the shop. It is so weathered and torn that it is quite illegible, the very opposite of the primly vertical poster in the vitrine on the right, whose figures are depicted in tones only slightly cooler than those of the wares on display.

The work's greatest appeal, however, lies not merely in the endless fascination observers may find in pursuing visual details of the *Rue des Saints Pères* and its shops. There is the fascination of a sharply receding vista that opens before us, even as it reveals nothing more than a tempting glimpse of nature. It does offer an irresistible contrast, the unexpected reward of discovering air, some openness and a bright shaft of light in the heart of a busy, crowded city. As if to celebrate its beauty, Pradzynski coyly provided a clue for the passerby: while the ironwork of the shuttered windows above the two shops is stark and unadorned, the corresponding decorative forms over the gateway leading to J. Martens' distant, but vivid red door boasts a garland that drapes downward, into the cold gray stone of a Paris whose antiquity, and, paradoxically, modernity, are boldly evoked.

In another work with an emphatic horizontal format, and strong frontality, *Le Café Vogue*, the shutters above the actual cafe have been thrown open carelessly, with their peeling paint hanging in tatters here and there, and the inner panels jut against one another to form an unusual, dynamic herringbone pattern. Curtains are closed in the adjacent windows, and the doors are shut, preventing the eye from wandering into the lobby and interior rooms. But between the wooden door and another shop, "Le Crequier," is an open doorway that offers compositional and emotional release from the impassive, geometric store fronts, a typical and subtle Pradzynski device. Just off center, is the "Passage Ste. Anne," marked by the bright red sign overhead and a powerful arch and curved window with a molding that together offset the massive masonry walls.

LE CAFÉ VOGUE
1998 ACRYLIC
18 X 42 INCHES (46 X 106 CM)

LIBRAIRIE P. DUVAL
1997 ACRYLIC
29 X 39.5 INCHES (73 X 100 CM)

Indeed, the very solidity of the walls, plastered long ago with stucco that now is falling away, makes the passageway all the more enticing. Although the vista is veiled by shadows, it appears to be washed with a welcome light. Like some hidden garden, the space beyond the painting's actual boundaries is implied, but then kept just out of reach in a somewhat tantalizing manner. The tiny, impenetrable space at the heart of Pradzynski's painting becomes all the more compelling because it stands in such sharp contrast to the rectilinearity and flatness of the Parisian street, however evocative.

There are no people in attendance at the moment in *Le Cafe Vogue*, but the Parisians rushing here and there in well-known period photographs by Brassai and Atget, or stopping for *un cafe* and a cigarette, do seem to be just around the corner, out of sight but not out of mind. The notion of a recent human departure, of the smoke or perfume that still lingers in a doorway or wafts down from a balcony, is woven into the very fabric of Pradzynski's Paris paintings, and a multitude of serigraph prints, even though his works have clear affiliations with the category of "still life," and have a very

considerable, satisfying power of their own without the human presence. One can also extrapolate the artist's experiences in Paris as an impressionable adolescent as well as his constant explorations of every corner of the city today in his search for motifs. There is no doubt that the sensory aspect of his works, and their evocative powers, remain peculiarly powerful, and personal, even though his subject matter steadfastly excludes the human form.

In *Librairie P. Duval*, for example, the familiar becomes novel, and then reverts to the familiar once again. The painting is named for a storefront rendered so realistically as to transcend the veracity of a photograph. His choice of motif is as mysterious as the scene he sets before his viewer: a shallow space dominated by two shops, each surmounted by a stuccoed arch broken by a window, vaguely suggesting a face articulated by emphatic eyebrows and veiled eyes. So much is detailed in *Librairie P. Duval*, yet so much remains just beyond the observer's ability to perceive.

Pradzynski positions himself and his imaginary viewer in the street outside the shops which appear dark, cavernous and somewhat intimidating in their somberness. The wares in their windows, however, engage our attention as an assortment of vividly realized objects, set on a flattened plane. They can be associated with the late 19th-century *trompe l'oeil* studies of the American masters of illusionistic painting, John Peto and William Harnett, or even with contemporary photo-realist paintings by Richard Estes, Audrey Flack and others. The mechanisms are similar: the use of a space too shallow to allow much penetration into the complex composition, the intense observation of unremarkable still life elements, including the wealth of fine detail in the windows of Pradzynski's shops, and the quiet, reflective mood induced by those seemingly random bits of life, cast into such sharp focus.

Yet the pictorial effect is strikingly different in each body of work. In Pradzynski's Paris studies, and particularly in *Librairie P. Duval*, the artist is at pains to produce with startling accuracy, apparently, something more atmospheric than the prosaic subject matter that appears before him. He clearly wants to inject with

increasingly subtle means, the objectification of what Paris itself allows him to feel, even if it is at times a kind of *nostaglie de la boue*, an unmistakable sympathy and identification with the least alluring, even disreputable streets of Paris and their urban texture. Pradzynski's sense of mission recalls the admittedly far more disturbing and fantastic work of the French Surrealists who generations earlier had exposed themselves to the urban experiences of Paris that might produce in them, as André Breton put it, "a lyrical substance." Pradzynski has repeatedly wandered the streets of Paris for years, seeking the particular vistas and facades that could be transformed into an appropriate urban landscape. His visual reports may appear persuasively actual, but they can also be understood as poetic constructs. Lyrical amalgams of several studies, in fact, aided and abetted by photography, they are freely compressed and edited to form a new, more intense and evocative reality. Typically, *Librairie P. Duval* is a new kind of still life on a grand scale, and yet it remains very personal.

William M. Harnett, United States, Alas, Poor Yorick, 1877,
Los Angeles County Museum of Art, CA, Gift of Charles C. and Elma Shoemaker

LA PORTE AU VITRAIL
1996 ACRYLIC
7 X 13 INCHES (18 X 33 CM)

However much his paintings may recall the world that Atget and Brassai knew so well, a world of frozen moments in time which the artist himself often enjoys reentering imaginatively and restudying, his intention is neither nostalgic reverie nor a calculated *trompe l'oeil* exposition that merely replicates Paris and its romantic imagery. Rather than being obsessed by the intrinsic charm, nostalgic associations or beauty of his views of old Paris, as if they were rare and valuable objects in themselves, Pradzynski was primarily interested in the effect of light even on the most banal signs, storefronts and architecture. Given the intensity of his perceptions and their unique pictorial results, one must conclude that he has, perhaps unconsciously, also drawn on his romantic boyhood memories and expectations of Paris, heightened as they were by sheer contrast with his apparent dismay upon returning to a kind of exile in Poland. This layering of memory and different time frames, with other less easily defined influences, gives Pradzynski's Parisian paintings an indefinable mystery and romantic resonance. Given the presence of these ancillary factors, one is sometimes tempted to invent imaginary scenarios for his paintings. In the painting *La Rue Mazarine* the viewer is automatically disposed to place it in some vaguely defined contemporary realm. At the same time, however, the past becomes as vital an element as the loosely defined present. The posters on the crumbling walls appear recent enough not to show signs of wear, while the larger sign beside them obviously dates from an earlier era. Its lettering is archaic, and the thinned washes of gray paint have gradually fallen away from the wall, which itself is in the process of eroding. Is there something going on in *La Rue Mazarine*, some action involving the abandoned bicycle rack, which itself resembles an old-fashioned hitching post, and perhaps the drab weathered doorway? Yet, while the work's enigmatic cluster of objects may hint at anecdotal content, some elusive and possibly thrilling scenario, they never coalesce into a readily definable narrative content.

Most viewers perceive the artist's pictorial reconstructions of Paris as both a delightful new and old world, filled with all the mystery, romance and pleasure that Pradzynski discovered there between 1960 and 1965, when he was free to wander and absorb the visual splendor of an artist's Paradise. The city that became his constant subject drew him back, and once he returned to Paris, it held his rapt attention. Gradually, patiently, he found a way to share that fascination with his audience. His first paintings of Paris were small, painterly and unassuming. As time passed, Pradzynski's vision became more assured, his attack more energetic and his style strongly individualized. But the essential elements remained, and became simply more expansive and liberated. They express his characteristic blend of opposites: the fine attention to detail that suggests the exquisite vision of numerous historical and modern masters, from the Northern Renaissance to Manet, but they also conjure up the bold, flickering hand of the vernacular street painter, tossing off one view of Paris after another. Ancient and contemporary influences are absorbed and reconstituted, playing off one another, and creating poetic, allusive sparks.

Pradzynski's works comment subliminally on the nature of time, and even life itself, despite the absence of the human form or concrete anecdote. He lures the viewer into his world, which recreates down to the finest detail the Paris he knows by heart. He then sets the viewer free to wander in an urban landscape so idealized, so deftly composed and personalized, that it might as well be a still life. The subject is Paris, and yet it is not; in fact, it is the artist's particular Paris, a Paris of the mind that has evolved over a long period and that continues to evolve today in unpredictable visual inventions. His evolutionary process is voracious, factoring in everything from vintage photographs to memory, mood and even the passing moment, the experience, perhaps, of that morning's walk. Then, as the artist recently told the author, he proceeds "to manipulate everything." He shapes his reality as a sculptor might, blending and smoothing all elements into a whole that is more real than reality, lending verisimilitude even to the most potentially disjunctive elements.

LA PORTE BLEUE
1996 ACRYLIC
7 X 13 INCHES (18 X 33 CM)

La Porte Verte

1996 Acrylic

7 x 13 inches (18 x 33 cm)

LE GARAGE LECLERC
1999 ACRYLIC
32 X 45.5 INCHES (81 X 115 CM)

LE LIBR' ENFANT
1997 ACRYLIC
18 X 42 INCHES (46 X 106 CM)

LA PRESIDENCE
1997 ACRYLIC
29 X 46 INCHES (73 X 116 CM)

PORTE BLEUE RUE STE. ANNE
1996 ACRYLIC
46 X 32 INCHES (116 X 81 CM)

VINS DU MONDE
1997 ACRYLIC
24 X 32 INCHES (60 X 81 CM)

LOUIS BOUTON TAPISSIER
1998 ACRYLIC
32 X 39 INCHES (81 X 99 CM)

LES DEUX LIBRAIRIES
1996 ACRYLIC
32 X 46 INCHES (81 X 116 CM)

PASSAGE L'HOMME II
1999 ACRYLIC
36.5 X 20 INCHES (92 X 50 CM)

VENEZIA

T homas Pradzynski's Parisian scenes are so successful in their resolution of formal and anecdotal elements, and so richly evocative of a particular urban locale that one might imagine only the Paris venue could inspire his distinctive approach. Yet his subsequent, and overlapping series of Venetian paintings have proven equally ingenious pictorially and insinuating in sentiment, taking his romantic treatment to even more complex levels. The kind of painstaking observation evident in the Paris paintings has also been brought to bear in his painting *Via Della Colonna* of 1990 and *Accademia S. Marco*, a small painting executed in 1997 that explores every crevice of the faded red wall adjoining the academy stairway.

Pradzynski's characteristic blending of past and present is as subtle in these works as in any he created in the greyed and nuanced light of Paris, drawing on the more unified elements of architecture and the more sanguine mood Venice no doubt inspired. Influenced perhaps by the landscapes of Canaletto and other 18th-century "vedutists," as well as by the golden light and radiant atmosphere of the unique city itself, the artist applied his thin acrylic washes with a conspicuous exhilaration, and in due course he was inspired to embark on an even more daring course of pictorial experimentation.

DETAIL FROM CANAL GRANDE I

The vines that cling to crumbling walls in *Accademia S. Marco*, like the brightly high-lighted patch of peeling paint above the railing at the composition's far left, appear almost impressionistic in the looseness of their brush-work. Similarly, the mottled hues of the stippled stucco wall are given a refreshing vitality and breadth that accents the striking effect of sun-light on diverse surfaces. These vary from rough stone to smooth vines to the polished, gleaming rondels of the cames defining the latticework in the arched Islamic window.

Although it measures only eleven by sixteen inches, this jewel-like painting suggests myste-rious interior spaces, with its glimpses through an open window, and even up an unseen staircase we can readily imagine leads to the studio behind the sign, "Accademia S. Marco." Here Pradzynski relied on the format that proved so effective in his studies of Parisian shopfronts, and which he continued to do in such brilliantly realized works as *Tiepolo*, *Liquori Vini* and *Vini da Pinto*. All three paintings are relatively flat, horizontal compositions taking full advantage of the colorful, sharp juxtapositions in color and form of neighboring buildings and vistas available to him in Venice. The abundance of monuments and picturesque vernacular archi-tectural forms provided a wealth of textural and tonal explorations in the extraordinary ambience of Venice, with its higher luminosity, airiness and brilliant, contrasting hues.

ACCADEMIA S. MARCO
1997 ACRYLIC
11 X 16 INCHES (27 X 41 CM)

VINI DA PINTO
1997 ACRYLIC
32 X 51.5 INCHES (81 X 130 CM)

The new source of inspiration is undoubtedly different from Paris, and perhaps proved more spiritually liberating. With its incomparable Piazza San Marco shimmering brightly in the lagoon, Venice evokes a more exotic range of associations than Pradzynski's magnificent Paris, a city he had personally explored and assimilated even before adolescence. The marvels and marbles, the churches and palaces, and the winding waterways of Venice have fascinated travelers since the Middle Ages. English gentlemen of the 18th century who embarked on the Grand Tour to complete their education made a mandatory stop in Venice, and artists came to admire the decaying grandeur of its monuments as well as masterpieces of the Venetian Renaissance, from Titian to Tintoretto, and the later, magnificent mural decorations of Tiepolo.

Quite apart from its historical interest and monuments, Venice today still provides a unique, surging energy and optical effects not found elsewhere in Europe. The city also casually offers countless picturesque souvenirs as tangible as the oily canals with the red skiff that bobs up and down invitingly in *Via Della Colonna*, yet somehow remains an elusive material reality. Given the theatrical setting and inexhaustible interest of Venetian architecture, from its palaces and churches to the humblest neighborhood square, or "campo," never very distant from the mysterious network of canals, this unique panorama, with its indigenous drama, creates an enchanted realm where myth and reality become one.

Giovanni Antonio Canaletto, 1697-1768, Piazza San Marco.
The Metropolitan Museum of Art, NY, Purchase, Mrs. Charles Wrightsman, Gift 1988.
(1988.162) Photograph © 1989 The Metropolitan Museum of Art

Pradzynski's oeuvre absorbed the Venetian past, actual and fanciful, and it became part of his world view as he sought to embrace a vast new subject. Venetian architecture is unique and often sublime, standing between East and West, stamped by centuries of stylistic influxes that contributed to its colorful ensemble: Roman, Byzantine, Moorish, Baroque and Gothic, with modern additions that reflect contemporary Italy. Just as Delacroix, the ultimate Romantic painter, saw his palette and subject matter explode when he visited North Africa almost two centuries ago, Pradzynski reacted to an almost overwhelming set of new ideas, images, lighting conditions, surface textures and perhaps most dramatically, to the violent colors of Venice, with a renewed passion that ignited his imagination.

LIQUORI VINI
1997 ACRYLIC
28.5 X 51.5 INCHES (72 X 130 CM)

TIEPOLO
1997 ACRYLIC
21.5 X 51.5 INCHES (54 X 130 CM)

Campo S. Giacomo da l'Orio
1997 Acrylic
11 x 9 inches (27 x 22 cm)

Apart from the unique setting, perhaps the colors of Venice have the strongest initial impact on the viewer. Sunlight, so intense that it borders on the unendurable, bathes the facades in *Tiepolo*, both the entrances to the reconstituted palazzo's art gallery where Tiepolo's paintings are on display as well as the shops and upper-level apartments that open not onto sidewalks, as they do in Paris, but abruptly and without transition onto canals. At the waterline a wide, dark band of water is visible, animated by low waves that shatter the reflected facades into complex patterns of ochre and blue-white passages splashed with touches of scarlet and cobalt. The effect is quite mesmerizing, and offers Pradzynski a pretext for lapidary passages of brushwork. With their classical arches and rhythmically repeated square openings, the solid building structures dissolve into vibrant zigzags and silken curls of paint that refer only obliquely to their origins, and through the artist's vivid depiction take on a life of their own.

Pradzynski creates in his Venetian series yet another kind of stage set void of the human form but, at the same time, so redolent of a recent or incipient incident that its anticipatory vacuum propels his viewer into a state of imaginative projection and sympathetic participation. What might otherwise appear to be an apparent paucity of ideas, or mistaken for a dutifully literal representation of an existing scene, set out pictorially in a static, frontal composition, is transformed by the integrity and subtleties of the artist's expressive intensity, his evident emotion and personal address to his subject matter. Even in romantic Venice the essence of his art remains the presentation of everyday things in the everyday world, with unwavering truthfulness. But there is also an undercurrent of emotion, already vital in the Paris series, and quite irresistible in the warmer, livelier paintings produced in Venice. Empty boats beckon, and deep loggias, like the one to the left in *Tiepolo*, draw the eye into their depths, luring the viewer into the romantic gloom, and inviting him to pass beyond mere fact into the unseen but intuitively experienced rooms beyond.

In much the same way, though in a more cheerful, uplifting motion, the eye sweeps through the arched passageway between the converted palazzo, whose banner touts what must be a current exhibition of works by Tiepolo, and the shop, Tarantola. The viewer's gaze is drawn up the sunlit stairway to a courtyard for tenants, a common where people may meet and enjoy the fragrant, unhurried pace of life in Venice, and the viewer's mind dwells on the fables that surround this unique locale.

The staircase, with its halo of light around and above it is a focal point of *Tiepolo*, and that may even be understood to emphasize transcendent implications. As he did to a lesser extent in his Parisian series, Pradzynski blurs the lines between past and present, the real and the imagined, allowing them to overlap and even coexist. He even suggests that this slice of Venice, with its horizontal expanse of facades, goes beyond the limited and specific subject matter, to embody the substance of the city, and all that it once was. There is a seductive mannered quality in the ephemeral staircase, giving it the architectural semblance of, and conceivably a connection with, the baroque staircases and architectural wonders of Bernini

and Borromini. Pradzynski's heightened emphasis on a visionary aspect of this scene injects a historical non-sequitur into his contemporary space, rather mysteriously recalling the past that is so much a part of Venice, with its powerful heritage apparent on all sides. The intensity of the light cascading down the banister to the narrow opening, partially blocked by an ornate balustrade in *Tiepolo*, does seem disproportionate to one's expectations of the stolid, seried blocks of buildings otherwise dominant.

The theatrical quality of the lighting on the staircase in *Tiepolo*, unlikely even in a brilliantly illuminated Venice, appears to be an arbitrary invention, an inexplicable *tour-de-force*. It makes sense, however, if we can perceive it as light on another plane, coming from another, more ancient Venice, inviting viewers to step into the past. We can imagine this light magically opening onto an atrium, in which flowers bloom with frescos on the surrounding walls, and fountains flow. Frivolous though such an interpretation might be, it seems plausible especially after a close scrutiny of Pradzynski's remarkable, multi-layered paintings which soon followed. The work, by design, requires a leap of faith.

At first glance his method seems deceptively simple, even mundane, but with more experience, we begin to plumb, and enjoy, its hidden depths. The content has much to do with both his pictorial methods and his freely transforming approach to his subject matter. Rather than merely wander in Venice and make sketches or photographs of its vistas, for his painting series, he allows his impressions to accumulate and overlap, to become layered like geological strata over time, or successive veils of pigment on an evolving canvas. For the artist, no single interpretation is more valid than another. What matters for Pradzynski is the aggregate, the overall emotion that the final, often complex work evokes, for himself and for the imaginative, receptive observer.

"The story I wished to tell about Venice was not complete until I arranged and layered my sketches into new compositions," he has said. In his initial forays into the twisting walkways that endlessly ring the canals of Venice, with its resonant overlays of history at every turn, Pradzynski retained the approach that he had refined in his Parisian paintings. As time passed, his concept became both more intuitive, and his approach more free, so much so that in 1997 he began to experiment with transfers of photomontage, adding richness to his surfaces and vastly extending his subject matter's range of references.

(PRECEEDING PAGES)

CANAL GRANDE I
1997 ACRYLIC & MIXED-MEDIA
69 X 45 INCHES (175 X 114 CM)

CANAL GRANDE II
1997 ACRYLIC & MIXED-MEDIA
69 X 45 INCHES (175 X 114 CM)

CANAL GRANDE III
1997 ACRYLIC & MIXED-MEDIA
69 X 45 INCHES (175 X 114 CM)

CANAL GRANDE IV
1997 ACRYLIC & MIXED-MEDIA
69 X 45 INCHES (175 X 114 CM)

(FOLLOWING PAGE)

CORTE ZANETTI
1997 ACRYLIC & MIXED-MEDIA (TRIPTYCH)
46 X 81.5 INCHES (116 X 207 CM)

VRBIS

CORTE

His pictorial advances are dramatically evident in the four large-scale paintings, entitled *Canal Grande I — IV*, which resulted from a bold new technique and fresh experimental efforts. The canvases are divided into three sections: the top of the intricate composition shows former private palazzos, often of singular architectural beauty, and now well-known as public museums and cultural institutions which line Venice's main waterway, the Grand Canal. Along the bottom of these large canvases extends a decorative frieze of vignettes of garden ornament and small architectural structures from unspecified sites. Set squarely in the center of each canvas are a mosaic of repeating decorative motifs, only dimly visible, in the form of architectural details of Moorish or Byzantine window frames. These pale but dominant motifs are covered with layers of whitish, transparent paint, which suggest a fog rolling in from the lagoon, virtually obliter-ating solid form. At the center of each canvas, adding yet another psychological twist and radical shift in scale, are enlarged images of decorative sculptured heads, male and female, resembling garden statuary. The photomontage

PORTA DI VENEZIA
1997 ACRYLIC & MIXED-MEDIA (TRIPTYCH)
24 X 54 INCHES (61 X 137 CM)

transfers are reminiscent to some degree of Rauschenberg's silkscreened imagery taken from photojournalism, and these juxtapositions add a startling but fresh contemporary note to Pradzynski's historical reminiscences.

VIA S. ANTONIO
1997 ACRYLIC
11 X 18 INCHES (27 X 46 CM)

His other Venetian paintings focus on the diurnal and ordinary, and confirm his refined skill in what an American artist of another era, Edwin Blashfield, once cogently described as "the art of making the necessary beautiful." [4] In *Liquori Vini*, a trio of flame-arched lancet windows amplify in much larger scale some of the features of the smaller study, *Accademia S. Marco*. The windows are subtly balanced just off center and, significantly, they call attention to the post-and-lintel doorway below, and through it, a vista into a courtyard lost in dappled shadow. The appeal of the larger work is positively operatic, by contrast, as *Liquori Vini* abstracts from the smaller study to build a composition filled with richer references.

Once again, we discern symbols of the past and present, which come together in the contrasting shop signs; one represents an antiques dealer and the other, on a note both prosaic and piquant, a liquor store. The antiquities are in deep shadow, as if submerged behind layers of history; the wine-and-spirits shop, by contrast, presents a lively set of masterful *trompe l'oeil* vitrines, jammed with an assortment of bottles over which light plays lovingly, handsomely as it might in classic 17th-century Caravaggesque still life.

While *Liquori Vini* takes its compositional expertise from its Parisian prototypes, the painting develops its own kind of wit and a special personality. It is part of an ongoing series, certainly, and shares key characteristics with the artist's earlier concepts and those that followed in the recent group of Naples paintings. Carefully and cleanly constructed, the painting approaches geometric purity with its rectangular format, stark planes and sharp edges. But the pattern of weathering, especially in the bleached spots on the facade above the stores, and the softer brushstroke defining those areas create something like the broken, permeating light of an early French Impressionist work. *Liquori Vini* shares Pradzynski's concern for an all-inclusive, multi-faceted imagery. The painting of a neglected corner of Venice where a layer of bricks from another century are visible beneath stucco that seems almost equally hoary, combines the compositional devices he has mastered as well as actual replications of details from other related works in the series, among them the memorable *Accademia S. Marco*.

Like the sly, playful juxtapositions of his Paris series, the Venice paintings cleverly toy with visual reality, and with time-honored painterly techniques for creating their simulacrum. In *Liquori Vini* the artist has devised a kind of "metaphysical" style of realism very much his own, where fact and fancy, past and present interact convincingly, and at the same time serve as a metaphor for Pradzynski's subtle control of pictorial fact. He has combined a meticulous realism with the arbitrary juxtaposition of unrelated objects, or incompatible vistas. At the same time he has gained significantly in various skills, attaining more spontaneity and directness, and demonstrating a greater ability to record his refined impressions with immediacy and credibility. Though he still limits his dominant motifs to a horizontal format and strict frontality, relying on an abstracted and highly decorative patterning in a smoothly detailed technique, we are free to appreciate more fully the subtle evidence of intelligence and warmth in the play of light and softer modeling of his continually evolving painting series.

CAMPO S. TOMA
1997 ACRYLIC
16 X 13 INCHES (41 X 33 CM)

LA FINESTRA VERDE
1997 ACRYLIC
9.5 X 6 INCHES (24 X 15 CM)

Even the most overtly non-naturalistic elements in transitional paintings such as *Liquori Vini* and another signal painting of 1997, *Vini da Pinto*, became contributing elements in the most accomplished works of the Venetian series, chief among them the triptych *Sotoportego* and the poignant and beautifully executed *Canal Grande IV*, both dated 1997. The three sections of *Sotoportego* read as a continuous horizontal facade, with two landscapes, each providing a passageway into an indeterminate depth, separated quite abruptly by a central panel overpainted with a photo transfer. This translucent veil of thinned white pigment only faintly reveals the ghostlike details of a metal balustrade and repeating window openings of the clearly articulated, colorful facades flanking the sides of the center panel with sharply focused colorful detail of doorways and windows. Despite its obscuring mass of white fog, the middle panel redefines elements and vistas from each side panel: an ornate, curving balcony railing is repeated, as if some kind of visual stuttering were in progress, and the whiplash design from another railing, apparently upside down, also recurs in altered form, suggesting a dream atmosphere.

Whatever the explanation or intention, this complex visual document makes a fascinating study with its wealth of suggestive detail, and the concept is intellectually appealing. Pradzynski explored variations on similar themes in his more inventive compositions built around the theme of Venetian architecture, and, by implication, Venetian history. *Canal Grande IV* perhaps best exemplifies his progress toward an integration of his earlier approaches. He restates deliberately truncated and reassembled ghostly fragments, which are encouraged to coalesce into a new and fully coherent visual statement. Each of the four-part painting series is relatively large, measuring four by six feet, and when hung together, the complex attains an impressive mural scale. It combines some of the loveliest romantic fragments of a city that is celebrated for its picturesque beauty and ever-changing landscape. The end result of the experiment is more than merely cumulative, as the paintings reach a new level of synthesis that concentrates the mind as well as the eye.

Instead of spreading out his architectural and decorative still life elements in separable, sequential combinations, or playing with their dimensions and details, Pradzynski has sought a more ambitious synthesis. His four large canvases dedicated to the Grand Canal allow Pradzynksi to tell a more compact story, by creating a pictorial whole greater than the sum of its parts. Once again this series demonstrates his uncanny control of allusive, emotionally charged material. In *Canal Grande IV*, a prime example, the upper register depicts a Venetian street scene, with crumbling *palazzi* capturing the last ruddy rays of the day, and a lone white barque awaiting a passenger. The bottom section is even more moody and elegiac, although non-committal about a specific incident or historical moment in time. Contrasting with the bright and clear atmosphere at the top of the canvas, the white mist of the photo transfers physically and spatially dominate the ensemble, while the eroding classical statuary and garden "folly" below may suggest a marginally dispiriting mausoleum for some viewers.

The colors that were bright, vivid and actual in the upper register have bled away below, leaving only diminished hues resembling an old hand-colored tintype, and perhaps hinting at the subtle, sad changes wrought by time's passing. As if to support the mood of wistful nostalgia, the broad central section of *Canal Grande IV* echoes the middle panel of *Sotoportego* in its tripartite structure, a format that itself evokes the classicizing regularity of Venetian architecture. Replete with ornate stonework, in a pattern repeated in overlays of the photo transfers, the heart of the work has been veiled with a thin coat of white acrylic paint that cunningly reveals more than it conceals.

PALI AZZURI
1997 ACRYLIC
11 X 18 INCHES (27 X 46 CM)

SOTOPORTEGO DEI BISATI
1997 ACRYLIC
16 X 13 INCHES (41 X 33 CM)

Indeed, the subtle veiling effect actually focuses the mind, requiring special attention by repetition of what is almost hidden, as Pradzynski develops his allusive tendencies and continued fascination with the passage of time and life's transience. Then, in a gesture that has an air of grandeur but continues the note of pathos, he punctuates the canvas that veers between vague and explicit, between today and some forgotten yesterday, and a host of other complex associations, with a rather touching image of statuary in the form of an uplifted face wearing a beatific, otherworldly expression. Actually it is difficult to interpret or even to make out the eroded features, or to place them in an historical context. Is the haunting visage the ruin of a baroque angel worthy of Bernini, or a contemporary grave-yard monument, closer to kitsch?

No matter; the face becomes for Pradzynski the intersection of past and present, and anchors a dazzling kaleidoscope of images on both of the painting's two carefully demarcated levels above and below, all within a quite spectacular collage. This bold Venetian sequence may seem to flirt with disaster at first sight, with its visual dissonances and unexpected oppositions, but it triumphs finally as a touching, nostalgia-driven but utterly captivating *tour-de-force*.

Trattoria alla Palazzina
1997 Acrylic
11 x 18 inches (27 x 46 cm)

NAPOLI

I n his recent, and in many ways most intricate, painting series dedicated to the city of Naples, Pradzynski has skillfully extended the allusive, mixed-media techniques with which he experimented in his most striking evocations of Venice. The new Naples paintings take the complex methodology, and the corresponding mythology of that series, and move them in other appropriate directions, mixing memories and nostalgia with contemporary fact. At the root of the mix in the current Naples series are symbolic as well as actual elements that go beyond the *trompe l'oeil* borders of his most experimental Venetian paintings. He has also begun working more freely, loosening his brushstrokes and using a more sophisticated technique in a more overtly challenging manner, as he intertwines past and present, and immerses visual fact in emotional innuendo.

The greater freedom of invention in his more venturesome Naples series also involves a willingness to reveal his underlying structures, mechanisms and intention. Here he has literally lifted the translucent veils that were palpable presences, but only partially revealed in his Venetian works. He has now taken a further step, allowing his overlapping planes and, by implication, overlapping dimensions of time to be clearly apprehended. In works from the new series, he expands on his use of applied images — posters or ancient shop signs, for the most part — by making his pivotal, realistic vista function as yet another "applied" visual element.

FRUTTI DI NAPOLI
1999 ACRYLIC & MIXED-MEDIA
39 X 39 INCHES (99 X 99 CM)

The effect is initially perplexing, as if Pradzynski took his first steps into overlapping historical eras and resurrected imagery from the past, with its complex associations, and began using it to undermine what appeared to be the realistic landscape itself, which in turn was relegated to a lesser status in the pictorial hierarchy as merely a new kind of design element. The main focus and central image in *Trattoria Napoletana*, for example, is a short expanse of shop fronts that closely resemble those in the Parisian and Venetian series. The vista in this ensemble, however, stops short of its frame. It appears to be on a canvas too small to reach all the way to the stretcher and, even more mysteriously, the underlying imagery references a fresco element extracted from Pompeii or Herculaneum.

These visual quotations are fragments couched in the recognizable visual idiom of the so-called "Second Style" paintings from the 1st century B.C. at the Villa Boscoreale, not far from present-day Naples. The subtle anterior references can be considered the ostensible subject of Pradzynski's novel and more complex series. His mundane urban study looks almost naturalistic enough to be glimpsed from an actual window, but it works on other levels, figuratively, perhaps as a window in art connecting us to the distant past and a continuing tradition.

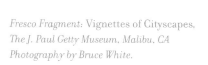

Fresco Fragment: Vignettes of Cityscapes.
The J. Paul Getty Museum, Malibu, CA
Photography by Bruce White.

TRATTORIA NAPOLETANA
1999 ACRYLIC
39.5 X 39.5 INCHES (99.5 X 99.5 CM)

VIA DELLE VERGINI
1999 ACRYLIC
32 X 45.5 INCHES (81 X 115.5 CM)

Structures are stacked one above the other, their exquisitely detailed surfaces criss-crossing each other as buildings may appear to the eye when seen fleetingly, in passing. With the Boscoreale fresco, however, gates, walls and villas are a jumble that becomes still more confusing, and still more theatrical upon closer scrutiny. The shops and passageway in *Trattoria Napoletana*, by contrast, are set in a precise row, one beside the next, as if presenting viewers with a logical panorama in an almost photographic overview which is undoubtedly their source. The illusionism in the Boscoreale frescos, however, is only approximate, as the basics of perspective were not understood until the Italian Renaissance, 1300 years after Vesuvius buried the villas of Pompeii and its environs in a suffocating, protective blanket of ash. By contrast, the illusionism of Pradzynski's vivid, if attenuated street scene is quite masterful in its understanding of perspective, and entirely convincing visually, as a credible slice of contemporary life minus the city's inhabitants, or any direct record of their existence.

What further reduces the credence of its *trompe l'oeil* triumph is the unsettling awareness that the urban vista is itself an alternative reality, by comparison with history, and that it might have been recreated from a guidebook color plate, or from a souvenir postcard. Its emphatically elusive nature, in other words, suggests that however realistic, however detailed the brilliant vista may appear, it could be interpreted as no more than another level of visual reality in a richly layered universe.

The two shops in *Trattoria Napoletana*, the hallway that divides them and the balconies and double-paneled doors overhead, offer other hints that they defy their connection to objective reality. The gold and jewelry in the windows of Leonardo Gaito are quite engagingly presented, rather like the astoundingly realistic calling cards and *billets doux* in still lifes by Peto or Harnett, and the facades appear at first glance picturesquely shabby.

In the Neapolitan series, the aging process has been accelerated to a level that is alarming; similarly, the saturated hues, visible brushwork and exaggerated shadows in *Trattoria Napoletana* and related works elicit not nostalgia but something bordering on anxiety. By pushing his naturalistic vehicle just beyond credible boundaries, Pradzynski ventures onto terrain barely explored in earlier series, tapping into a somewhat Surrealistic state that heightens his audience's ability to grasp his rich and deliberately evoked illusionistic strata. As if to force the issue, he underlines his fragmentary street scene in a register that combines realism with an obtrusive abstraction. A distracting shadow that also falls across the doorway of the trattoria takes on a dominant presence of its own as a competing, parallel reality. That band of gray, pale where the sunshine strikes it, and inky in the shadows, also works as a framing device, separating the realism of the shopfronts from the wall partially visible beneath the surface.

VILLA REALE
1999 ACRYLIC & MIXED-MEDIA
29 X 59 INCHES (73 X 149 CM)

CAFFÈ A. LAMBERTI
1999 ACRYLIC & MIXED-MEDIA
39.5 X 39.5 INCHES (99.5 X 99.5 CM)

On that level the barely legible imagery begins to look like poster paper recalling the half-remembered, somewhat intangible frescos of some ancient Roman villa. The gray band also acts as a disorienting, abstract, rectilinear form in a collage composed of a disparate group of objects: fading posters on peeling plaster walls and tourist picture postcards of Pompeii that show a partly draped nude, her reclining torso in a classical pose. There is no way to precisely pin down the images, nor to explicate concretely the meaning of the ensemble, much less of individual objects. With this potent series of intriguing, if disorienting visual references, as in some of his later Venetian studies, Pradzynski intends to evoke an emotional response rather than to communicate specific ideas.

Dreamlike in its vagueness, and seemingly random in the layering of unlikely forms and a confluence of paradoxical images, *Trattoria Napoletana* invites further speculation on a number of levels: formal, narrative and poetic. In much the same way, the paintings *Caffè A. Lamberti* and *Via della Luce* appear to be painterly collages loaded with mutually contradictory images in lushly textured, visually seductive form. They raise such puzzling and contradictory questions about reality itself that one must pause, and reflect on the further implications of these often rather arcane images and visual strategies. The key to Pradzynski's central metaphor lies not so much in the largest and most realistic component of each ensemble, that is, the cityscape, but rather in its borders. This manifold approach and mixed means, however, together elevate his most sustained achievement, that of rendering contemporary reality with an admirable exactness, from reportage to poetry.

Fresco Fragment: Woman on a Balcony
The J. Paul Getty Museum, Malibu, CA
Photography by Bruce White.

The Roman fresco motifs are profound markers, subtle yet specific references to the artist's reaction to Naples, Capri and the ancient cities they adjoin. The images of his recent Naples inventions produce ghostly, intriguing emanations from the Greco-Roman world — frescos from the Villa Boscoreale and elsewhere, art history's meager survivors of Vesuvius's eruption and the dessicating passage of time, Pradzynski has carefully explained to the author. These are references from our own history precious to the artist: images from an anterior age, depicting a populace at work and at rest, going about their daily activities. Even the arrangements of vivid, oversize fruits that decorate the upper margins of a number of recent Pradzynski paintings might have been reproduced from markets in a Roman forum, or found in an atrium that was lost long ago. To put it another way, they can also be equated with the contemporary poster shreds, peeling stucco and flaking painted advertisements on the walls of old Paris, and the misty shrouds dividing Venice's streets and gardens. They are artifacts, and sometimes brilliant *trompe l'oeil* references that may spark significant connections between present and past, between old and new, between true memory and romantic, poetic fictions.

This superb comparative device has become a familiar juxtaposition for Pradzynski, giving his work in all three of the great cities he has so assiduously investigated and portrayed a quality of psychological introspection, and considerable mystery. He offers us the romance of a secluded street, dappled by shadows and opening into a still more private, enclosed garden in *Via della Luce*. His visual clues are not quite as they appear: the patch of turquoise paint revealed under an eroding ochre on the gate into the courtyard is far more pristine and lively than anything that overlaid it as the ages moved on. Thus he suggests that what came before and was hidden, may after all be more valuable, more vibrant and enduring than our contemporary daubs. Similarly, the enormous portion of stucco that has fallen away from the wall over the sign, "Ceramica Casola," uncovers not lathe and plaster or even stone and other masonry materials but hints at what appears to be an ancient fresco.

VIA DELLA LUCE
1999 ACRYLIC & MIXED-MEDIA
39.5 X 39.5 INCHES (99.5 X 99.5 CM)

ISOLA D'ISCHIA
1999 ACRYLIC & MIXED-MEDIA
39.5 X 39.5 INCHES (99.5 X 99.5 CM)

The message is clear, and as revelatory as the moment in Fellini's great tribute to the ancient capital, Roma, when a construction crew breaks through to a long-buried room in a Roman villa. Caught up in the magic of the moment, willingly suspending disbelief at their great good fortune, some passersby enter the long-sealed room and gasp at the wonders they see, as no one had for 20 centuries: bright, fresh, joyous frescos. Then, to their collective horror, the moist, polluted air of modern Rome works its damage and the frescos fade, vanish and collapse into anguished memory. A similar spirit pervades Pradzynski's evocative Naples series, expressed not in the explicit style of Fellini's cinematic statement, or in real time, but more allusively, silently but with a kind of awesome serenity and conviction.

Like the *trompe l'oeil* masters of 19th-century American painting, Harnett and Peto, Pradzynski delights in his ability to mimic three-dimensional reality on a flat surface. Yet the facades and more complex overlays of visual reality that he has chosen to render with such startling versimilitude, only momentarily

transmit the sense of mundane reality so characteristic of their deliberately petrified 19th-century still lifes. Pradzynski's urban studies are essentially still lifes, too, but they have other dimensions in his own special kind of "virtual" reality. Even as he seems to be reducing whole vistas to fit into his highly selective, rather tense, geometric format, he is at once more arbitrary and free in his way of combining and manipulating photographs and other actual objects to fit his needs. His goal is multi-faceted in the luminous *Via della Luce*, another urban still life whose very name points to its lyrical, resonant subtext. Particularly in the large canvases from Venice and Naples, he admittedly works toward *trompe l'oeil* effects, seeking exactness within a structure approaching geometric purity at times. But it is not his intent to amaze or trick his viewer with his technical wizardry. He builds his naturalism on the time-honored rules of composition and technique, reinstating symmetry and the Golden Mean in a viable contemporary setting. He also pays attention to the classical forms and precepts of architecture, a calling which he once pursued, and whose vocabulary he assimilated in his own pictorial design.

The results of this complex history and apprenticeship are visually powerful, marginally philosophical and delightfully decorative in their interplay of light and form. He casts the pottery shop in *Via della Luce* into deep shadow, a pall as dense and dark as the ash that fell over Pompeii so long ago. The arbitrary shadow actually transforms the sidewalk in front of the ceramic shop into a kind of looming pit, on whose surface float disorienting bits of confetti-like, colored paper. In the shop windows themselves, as if emerging from some lost age, are the eternal ceramic vessels produced in the region since Greco-Roman times. Pradzynski always seems to be connecting past and present, almost inadvertently.

These implications also haunt the painting *Arancia*, one of his most complex and satisfying works with its multitude of perspectives, mingling the present moment, memories of a more heroic past, and dream. The oranges referenced by the painting's simplistic title are arranged in a row, as if on a narrow shelf, above a tripartite composition whose narrow verticality and compressed imagery focus on an arched entrance to a sunny courtyard. Like an arrangement of fruits and flowers in a Baroque still life by Zurburan or Cotán, or by the Dutch Little Masters whose mundane arrangements of flowers or food on a table were understood to comment on human mortality, Pradzynski's oranges are depicted in a variety of states: whole, sliced and partly peeled. They may or may not symbolize the stages of life, as the classic *memento mori* certainly do, but they certainly stand out dramatically for their narrative dissonance, and call attention to themselves not least of all for their brilliant execution.

VIA NARDONES
1999 ACRYLIC
21 X 32 INCHES (53.5 X 81 CM)

Arancia
1999 Acrylic & Mixed-Media
70.5 x 29 inches (179 x 73 cm)

Suspended in an indefinite, enveloping shadow above an urban landscape that in itself is a statement of simultaneous erosion, decay and renewal, their scale and convincing physical existence become odd, thought-provoking elements. On their own the fruits provide a sparkling, technically accomplished *trompe l'oeil* study. Assimilated to the Neapolitan passageway below, they can be perceived more as a flat, decorative border breaking the composition's logical format. But viewed in the work's fullest context, with the collage-like cluster of ancient fragments set in its lowest division, the band of oranges becomes talismanic, but also reassuring vis-a-vis contemporary reality. We can imagine the columns, arcade and frieze below as shadowy, fragile references tacked onto a bulletin board in architecture class to offer guidance in Vetruvian or Palladian theory. Contrasting with the crumbling real-life vista depicted in the middle of the painting, the historical reminiscences are relatively unmarked by the passage of time, and shown in sharply reduced scale, discontinuous with the other two sections of the riveting composition.

The three distinct sections of the painting, north and south, pull the narrative in seemingly incompatible directions. Yet the two major contradictions, at top and bottom, coexist with the contemporary scene without any sense of friction. Overall there is a settled sense of cool equanimity on the part of the artist. Whatever conflicts of subject matter, perspective and atmospherics may arise, they are ultimately integrated into a fresh interpretation of reality, as the artist strives for a greater universality by injecting his own consciousness into the pictorial equation.

Pradzynski is drawn to the anecdotal markers of a picturesque past within his own favored scheme of representational painting which he has aptly described as "poetic realism." Unlike the grand architecture and artifacts devised by the ancients that once promised eternal persistence, his intensely realized and vital, everyday objects themselves retain an uncanny power, outdoing the historical columns, temple and mural fragments that appear as a kind of bracketed, historical "quotation" in the lower section of *Arancia*. And in keeping with his own appreciation of life's simpler virtues, Pradzynski seems to be saying through his intense and skillful representation of a contemporary reality, alongside his persuasive montages of past and present, that these indispensable objects of everyday life are not only entirely natural but, for the artist, a source of enduring beauty and profound aesthetic satisfaction.

AGENZIA VENDITE EDITORE
1999 ACRYLIC & MIXED-MEDIA
39.5 X 22 INCHES (100 X 56 CM)

FABBRICA ARGENTERIA
1999 ACRYLIC & MIXED-MEDIA
39.5 X 22 INCHES (100 X 56 CM)

CORTILE NO. 20
1999 ACRYLIC
13 X 9 INCHES (33 X 22 CM)

FABBRICA DI CONFETTURE
1999 ACRYLIC & MIXED-MEDIA
39.5 X 22 INCHES (100 X 56 CM)

LA CASA DELLE UOVA
1999 ACRYLIC & MIXED-MEDIA
39.5 X 22 INCHES (100 X 56 CM)

CATALOGUE RAISONNÉ

Mastering the increasingly popular medium of printmaking through his sensitive but also precise explorations of silkscreen prints, or serigraphs, Thomas Pradzynski has brought a fresh romantic vision to the urban topography of Paris, Venice and Naples in his new body of work. Whether they be the dignified shopfronts of old Paris, the shimmering canals and rich mosaic of Venetian architecture, or the dilapidated alleyways of Naples, Pradzynski's facades are extraordinary in their balance of compact physical detail and meditative mood. He has become increasingly masterful in manipulating printers' inks, as he does paint itself, which may vary from thick to thin impasto. Despite the overall clarity of the work, his prints reveal the artist's great reverence for their weathered, time-worn subject matter.

Perhaps emulating the recognized masters of contemporary art such as Robert Rauschenberg and well-known realists and Pop artists Hockney, Lichtenstein and Warhol, Pradzynski has kept pace with contemporary printmakers. Their work in limited-edition prints maintains a level of creativity comparable to their unique paintings in oils and acrylics. While original paintings by well-known artists such as Pradzynski are relatively expensive to acquire, the immediacy and individuality of contemporary printmaking now bring the printmaker's art within the economic range of almost every art lover. New technologies of printmaking have helped open esthetic experience to a vast new public, as the syntax of the graphic mediums has been enthusiastically adopted by the serious painters of our time.

DETAIL FROM "PASSAGE VOLTAIRE"

SAN FRANCISCO
1994 SERIGRAPH

NEW YORK
1994 SERIGRAPH

PASSAGE VOLTAIRE
1994 SERIGRAPH

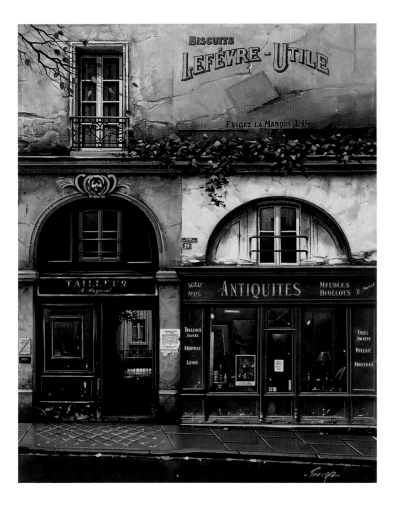

BOUTIQUE D'ANTIQUITES
1995 SERIGRAPH

PASSAGE VALMY
1995 SERIGRAPH

La Belle Epoque
1995 Serigraph

LA CAFETIÈRE
1995 SERIGRAPH

LES DEUX BANCS
1995 SERIGRAPH

SALON DE THÉ
1995 SERIGRAPH

VILLA D'ANVERS
1995 SERIGRAPH

FABRIQUE DE JOUETS
1995 SERIGRAPH

NAPOLI
1995 SERIGRAPH

VENEZIA
1996 SERIGRAPH

CAFE GITANA, ROMA
1996 SERIGRAPH

MATTINO NAPOLI
1996 SERIGRAPH

VILLA DES ROSIERS
1996 SERIGRAPH

IMPASSE DES TROIS FRÈRES
1996 SERIGRAPH

LA VIEILLE PROVENCE
1996 SERIGRAPH

CAFE PAUL
1996 SERIGRAPH

LA COUR DE COMMERCE
1996 SERIGRAPH

Le Bateau Lavoir
1996 Serigraph

PASSAGE DU CAIRE
1996 SERIGRAPH

RUE ST. ANNE
1996 SERIGRAPH

City of Paris Suite

Cour St. Antoine
1996 Serigraph

Les Toits de Paris
1996 Serigraph

L'EPICERIE
1996 SERIGRAPH

FABRIQUE DE FAIENCE
1997 SERIGRAPH

VILLA RIMBAUD
1997 SERIGRAPH

La Cour St. Hilaire
1997 Serigraph

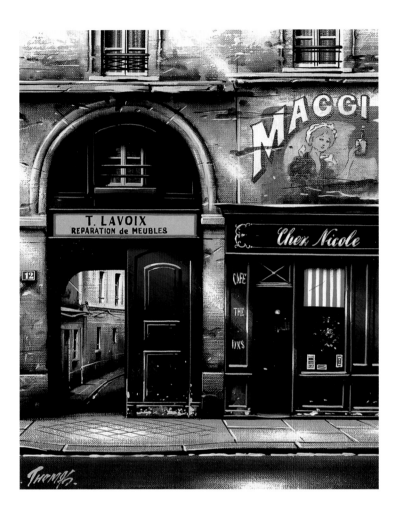

CHEZ NICOLE
1997 SERIGRAPH

GALERIE DE MAISTRE
1997 SERIGRAPH

JOSETTE FLEURISTE
1997 SERIGRAPH

Caffé Poggi
1998 Serigraph

Passage Choiseul
1998 Serigraph

Aïda
1998 Serigraph

Canali di Venezia Suite

CANALE GRANDE
1998 SERIGRAPH

CORTILE DI VENEZIA
1998 SERIGRAPH

VILLA BOCQUET
1998 SERIGRAPH

La Crémerie
1999 Serigraph

G. RENARD SALON DE THÉ
1999 SERIGRAPH

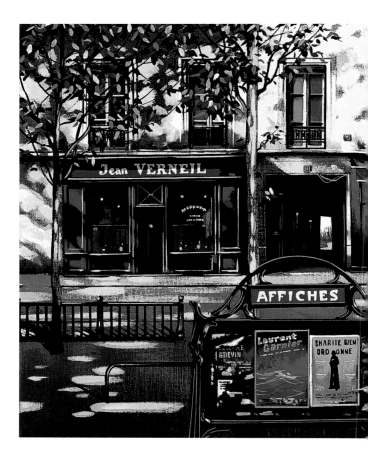

BOULEVARD JEAN VERNEIL
1999 SERIGRAPH

FABRIQUE DE CHAPEAUX
1999 SERIGRAPH

PASSAGE DU CHERCHE MIDI
1999 SERIGRAPH

FRUTTI DI NAPOLI

1999 SERIGRAPH

PRINT INDEX

Reminiscences Suite

City of Paris Suite

Passages de Paris Suite

Fenêtres de Paris Suite

Publisher's name printed on the lower right corner
of each edition.

Classic Edition Size:
200 numbered examples and 25 artist proofs

Deluxe Edition Size:
150 numbered examples and 25 artist proofs

RUE
DU PONT
LOUIS-PHILIPPE

RESTAURANT CA

RESTAURANT CHEZ J

PAINS
FRANÇAIS
VIENNOIS

CAFE BAR
Chez Julien

degustation

torrefaction
CAFÉ
Poggi

Glossary

Edition: The number of prints pulled, numbered and signed by the artist. Each edition may consist of Arabic numbered impressions, artist's proofs, *hors commerce* proofs, printer's proofs, trial proofs, presentation proofs, or any combination thereof. The denominator (lower number) indicates the size of the edition, the numerator (upper number) the sequence in which the impressions were signed. The Arabic numbered impressions are signed by the artist and consecutively numbered (e.g., 1/150, 2/150, 3/150...150/150). The artist's proofs (AP) are impressions outside the Arabic numbered edition, are signed by the artist and consecutively numbered (e.g., AP 1/25, AP 2/25...AP 25/25). The printer's proofs (PP) are impressions outside the Arabic numbered edition, are signed by the artist and consecutively numbered (e.g., PP 1/5, PP 2/5...PP 5/5). They are usually reserved for the printers. Presentation proofs and/or trial proofs are impressions outside the Arabic numbered edition and used by the publisher as presentation examples for the trade. *Hors Commerce* proofs are impressions outside the Arabic numbered edition, are signed by the artist and consecutively numbered (e.g., HC 1/10, HC 2/10...HC 10/10). They are usually reserved for the publisher.

Serigraphy: One of the four major divisions of fine art printmaking; commonly referred to as silk-screen printing. A serigraph print is made by a stencil technique using fabric (silk or synthetic) stretched tightly over a frame. The nonprinting areas on the fabric are blocked out by adhering a stencil. The image areas are porous fabric through which ink or paint is forced with a squeegee. The paper to be printed is placed on the table, the screen is placed on top, ink is applied through the screen openings directly to the paper. The name "serigraph" was coined in the United States for silkscreen prints made in the late 1930's. Anthony Velonis, credited for the name and much of the new interest in the medium, was a painter, graphic designer and the leader of the federally sponsored art project for screen printing under the Works Project Administration (WPA).

BIBLIOGRAPHY

Hughes, Robert. *Shock of the New.* Alfred Knopf, 1981.

Janson, H.W. *History of Art.* Harry N. Abrams Publishers, 1974.

Levin, Gail. *Edward Hopper, The Art and the Artist.* Norton/Whitney Museum, 1980.

Milner, John. *The Studios of Paris.* Yale University Press, 1988.

Perl, Jed. *Paris without End: On French Art since World War I.* North Point Press, 1988.

Notes: 1   Oliver Caldwell and Susan Snyder with Ralph Musco, *Thomas Pradzynski:*

Modern Realist, (San Francisco: Caldwell Snyder Publishing, 1993), pp. 30-31.

2   Op. Cit., p. 33.

3   Ibid., p. 27.

4   S. Lane Faison, *Handbook of the Collection,* (Williamstown, MA: Williams College

Museum of Art, 1979), Example 47, n.p.